I0412842

The Double-Edged Sword of Freedom of Speech

By Stanislaw Sielicki

Sielicki's Singles Series

Copyright © 2012 Stanislaw Sielicki

All rights reserved

ISBN: 1-4681-7890-3
ISBN-13: 978-1-4681-7890-6

DEDICATION

To Denis

CONTENTS

ACKNOWLEDGMENTS

I'd like to thank those who have been participating in *tête-à-têtes* and online discussions which inspired this essay: Denis and Nataly Sielicki, Alexey Kravchenko, Nikita Kasay, Lawrence Perepolkin, Alexandr Bibik, Andrey Cherepanov, Guy Payne, William Fisher, Igor Rozhkevich, Sergey Bogacki, Alexandre Roubtsov, Konstantin Novik, Denis Loginov, Carl Farber and Dmitry Chipiga.

Additional thanks go to Peter Guess, who edited the essay.

THE HYPOCRISY OF FREEDOM OF SPEECH

For the last few decades, our foreign policy has widely utilized a paradigm of advocating an absolute primacy of free speech and press as a very powerful propaganda weapon in the ideological wars against nations we wanted to crush. Namely, the Soviet Union, Cuba, Iraq, Yugoslavia, North Korea, and Libya; now Iran's "problem" is on the table. The free-speech-preaching policy has proven to be an ultimate weapon, against which there exists no defense. Regardless of how justified, reasonable, or minor these restrictions on freedom of speech were, defending them looked weak and unconvincing, and was always a losing strategy.

However, the unabridged free speech advocacy is destructive not only for those who are on its receiving end, but also for those who wield the weapon. The attacking side can easily become self-hypnotized into believing in the truthfulness and sincerity of the message, or even worse, experience a schizophrenic personality split, when one side of its public consciousness praises freedom of speech for an external use, and the other, at the same time, tries to find loopholes such as "hate speech", ethical concerns, and child protection, to limit it domestically or to excuse allies' actions.

Hypocrisy is not the answer to the dilemma of consolidating these two voices in the mind of the public—it leads to a moral corruption and, eventually, to an abandonment of all ideals. We have either to acknowledge, on the conceptual level, that the censorship and self-censorship of speech and press are no less important instruments of democracy than are the freedom of speech and press, or to throw away all these encroachments on the unabridged freedom of speech.

ANCIENTS AND FOUNDERS

At the dawn of democracy in Ancient Greece, philosophers recognized an utmost need for censorship and moral policing for the very survival of virtuous republics. Plato, in his "Republic", the apology of Socrates who was executed by the people of Athens for alleged corruption and perversion of the morals of the youth, shows that two lower classes of a society, the commoners and warriors, need a higher, ruling and educating class, which would impose and maintain the moral norms it created. These norms have to be strictly imposed by the moral policing, censorship, ostracism, and mutual surveillance and reporting of one citizen of the lower class to another. However, the higher class has to be excluded from these practices, because the very act of lawgiving needs a noble law-breaking.

In the first picture of an ideal city, which, in Plato's narrative, Socrates draws before his students, there exists only a lower class, a class of artisans (in the widest meaning of the word) of various crafts who have only basic material desires and live simple, almost

Rousseauist lives, in which there is place neither for greed nor courage. This picture neither satisfies his students, nor takes into account other possibly hostile cities.

For military occupation, a completely different class is needed, a class interested not in self-preservation, but in achievements of "spiritedness", even at the cost of life—the class of warriors; the class of guard dogs. But these dogs have to be trained to preserve and defend that which is theirs, and to viciously tear apart that which is the enemy. And another, the third class of philosophers, has to give the warriors law to obey.

However, these dogs know no reason why these laws were created, they recognize no exceptions, and, if left alone or allowed to acquire too much power, may mistake the free thinkers for enemy agents and turn on their masters. Therefore, a very strict moral policing with heavy penalties has to be enforced, with the shadow power of the literally "nocturnal council" which will oversee all aspects of private life, or even eliminate any possibility of citizens having any. (Republic 369–445)

Influence of the Classical thought on the Framers of the Constitution was substantial. Benjamin Rush, not a very well-known signatory of the Declaration of Independence and delegate of the Constitutional Congress, proposed a literally Spartan model for the new educational system:

> *Let our pupil be taught that he does not belong to himself, but that he is public property. Let him be taught to love his family, but let him be taught, at the same time, that he must*

forsake, and even forget them, when the welfare of his country requires it.

He must watch for the state as if its liberties depended upon his vigilance alone… These are practicable lessons, and the history of the commonwealth of Greece and Rome show that human nature, without the aids of Christianity, has attained these degrees of perfection.

*In the education of youth, let the authority of our masters be as **absolute** as possible… By this mode of education, we prepare our youth for the subordination of laws and thereby qualify them for becoming good citizens of the republic. I am satisfied that the most useful citizens have been formed from those youth who have never known or felt their own wills till they were one and twenty years of age, and I have often thought that society owes a great deal of its order and happiness to the deficiencies of parental government being supplied by those habits of obedience and subordination which are contracted at schools.*

(Rush 684–86, 689)

Those Founders who were not so enchanted by the Classical legacy were still taking it very seriously, spending quite a lot of time and effort battling Ancient concepts, professor of political science at the University of Toronto, Thomas L. Pangle notes:

The Founding generation's posture toward the classical republican tradition mingles real respect and some serious attachment with criticism so severe as to suggest a sense of alienation. The most reflective of the Founders take the classics too seriously, and struggle with them too intensely, to have regarded them simply from an "aesthetic" point of view.

(Pangle & Pangle 1993, 35)

ENLIGHTENMENT THINKERS AND FOUNDERS

Of course, the most illuminating revelation for the Framers was the body of works by European political thinkers of the Enlightenment Age. Among those who most inspired the Founding Fathers was John Locke, whose famous "pursuit of happiness" slogan found its way into the Declaration of Independence, and Charles-Louis Montesquieu, whom James Madison called "the Oracle".

Montesquieu, in his book *Considerations on the Causes of The Greatness of the Romans and Their Decline* praised the Roman mechanism of censorship:

> *I must mention a magistracy that greatly contributed to upholding Rome's government — that of the censors. They took the census of the people, and, what is more, since the strength of the republic consisted in discipline, austerity of morals, and the constant observance of certain*

customs, they corrected the abuses that the law had not foreseen, or that the ordinary magistrate could not punish. There are bad examples which are worse than crimes, and more states have perished by the violation of their moral customs than by the violation of their laws. In Rome, everything that could introduce dangerous novelties, change of heart or mind of the citizen, and deprive the state... of perpetuity, all disorders, domestic or public, were reformed by censors.

(Montesquieu 1999, 85–86)

Montesquieu pointed out that the homogeneous culture of Rome, with its political virtue of self-restraint and self-renouncement, was a cornerstone of the Roman success. When the Roman Empire expanded, the cultural values of conquered nations and their riches started diluting Roman morals, which eventually led to the decline of Rome:

When the domination of Rome was limited to Italy, the republic could easily maintain itself. A soldier was equally a citizen...

But when the legions crossed the Alps and the sea. The warriors, who had to be left in the countries they were subjugating for the duration of several campaigns, gradually lost their citizen spirit...

[Rome] therefore accorded to coveted right of citizenship to the allies... and gradually to all. After this, Rome was no longer a city whose people had a single spirit a single love of liberty, a single hatred of tyranny... each city

brought to Rome its genius, its particular interests... The distracted city no longer formed a complete whole. And since citizens were such only by a kind of fiction, since they no longer had the same magistrates, the same walls, the same gods, the same temples, and the same graves, they no longer saw Rome with the same eyes, no longer had the same love of country, and Roman sentiments were no more.

The ambitious brought entire cities and nations to Rome to disturb the voting or get themselves elected. The assembles were veritable conspiracies; a band of seditious men was called comitia. The people's authority, their laws and even the people themselves became chimerical things, and the anarchy was such that it was no longer possible to know whether the people had or had not adopted an ordinance.

(Montesquieu 1999, 92–93)

John Locke's ideas of the separation of Church and State, and how to build a future educational system for the country, were targeted, if you will, at indoctrination of the youth by democratic ideals. No surprise, therefore, that we may find the educational ideas of the Founders are still there in big part in today's American Educational System, with its prison-style discipline: everyday Pledge of Allegiance; total control over students' movement and—in big part—thought; detention practices and permanent student records; and are unnecessarily totalitarian and barbaric, especially from the Continental European's point of view.

Rush Welter, professor of American History at Harvard University, notes:

> *Early republican commitments to education ... are particularly striking to anyone who expects to discover a democratic orientation in the founding father's demands for a universal dissemination of knowledge ... many of the national plans for education emphasized the importance of instruction in common obligations to government and to the established institutions of society. Within the areas to which common agreement limited government, an informed obedience on the part of the people was at least as important as their particular freedom.*
>
> (Welter 1962, 27–28)

Indeed, those who had engineered, mastered and harnessed the dark and destructive forces of popular unrest to overthrow previous regime and climb up to the top, had to be very conscious about planting seeds of obedience in the population in order to avoid sharing the fate of the previous, more lay and unfortunate rulers.

ADVANTAGES OF THE
UNDEMOCRATIC CONSTITUTION

Alexander Hamilton, who wrote two thirds of the *Federalist Papers*, the ideological foundation of the Constitution project, was very doubtful about the ability of the general populace to manage their freedom coherently:

> *All communities divide themselves into the few and the many. The first are the rich and the well-born; the other the mass of the people ... turbulent and changing, they seldom judge or determine right. Give therefore to the first class a distinct, permanent share in the Government ... Nothing but a permanent body can check the imprudence of democracy.*
>
> (Hamilton 1985, 108)

This idea of a special role of elites as guides of a naive populace, and guardians of democracy, found its way into the Constitution in the form of giving the task of judicial review to the unbalanced, life-tenured Supreme Court and indirect Presidential and Senate elections. In "Federalist No. 78", Hamilton writes:

The independence of the judges is equally requisite to guard the Constitution ... from the effects of these ill humors, which the arts of designing men, or the influence of particular conjunctures, sometimes disseminate among the people themselves ... have a tendency ... to occasion dangerous innovations in the government... it would require an uncommon portion of fortitude in the judges to do their duty as faithful guardians of the Constitution, where legislative invasions of it had been instigated by the major voice of the community.
(Hamilton, Jay, Madison 2009, 347)

Anti-Federalist opposition voiced a strong critique of Hamilton, Madison and Jey's creation, calling it "Aristocratic Constitution", and mocking their "undercover" thinking, which would trample on peoples' liberties, earned in the Revolutionary War:

We have said nothing about a bill of rights, for we viewed it as an eternal clog upon our designs, as a lock chain to the wheels of government ... We have for some time considered the freedom of the press as a great evil — it spreads information, and begets a licentiousness in the people which needs the rein more than the spur; besides, a daring printer may expose the plans of government and lessen the consequence of our president and senate — for these and many other reasons we have said nothing with respect to the "right of the people to speak and publish their sentiments" or about their "palladiums of liberty" and such stuff. We do not much like that sturdy privilege of the people — the right to demand the writ of habeas corpus. We have therefore reserved the power of refusing it in cases of rebellion, and you know we are the judges of what is rebellion...

(Hamilton, Jay, Madison 2009, 433)

However, the elitist position of the Federalists has prevailed, and at the Constitutional Convention of 1887, the Bill of Rights was effectively removed from the project of the Federal Constitution by an astonishing unanimous vote of 10 to 0 (although, by that time, the Bill of Rights was an integral part of the Constitutions of the majority of States participating in the convention). But it did not prevail for long—only few years later, by 1891, it was pushed back into the Constitution by populist Congress.

In today's world, Hamilton's elitist argument is gaining more and more weight. Digital technologies accessible to everybody make it much easier to manufacture "ill humors", proliferate "influence of particular conjunctures", and "disseminate" them "among the people" who "seldom judge or determine right" much more effectively. And all of these for the benefits of "designing men", who may belong to a completely different culture to ours, and may have as a target an instigation of "dangerous innovations in the government".

Besides, of whom could Alexander Hamilton and his colleagues, the Undemocratic Founding Fathers, been afraid? There exists a popular, commonly accepted legend, especially within the Religious Right (represented, for example, by the works of Rob Gragg), regarding a so-called "Constitutional faith" of Americans. The spirit that brought "pilgrims"—the Calvinist, Puritan sects—into America, the spirit of searching for Liberty in the "religious oppression" of the official Anglican Church, whose head was the King of England, eventually lead to the uprising against the Crown, and the adoption of the Liberty-promoting Constitution.

Meanwhile, a typical Puritan statement formulating views on the government and belonging to John Cotton, one of principal ministers of the Massachusetts Bay Colony, sounds very totalitarian:

> *It is better that the commonwealth be fashioned to the setting forth of Gods house, which is the church: than to accommodate the church frame to the civil state. Democracy, I do not conceyve that ever God did ordeyne as a fitt government eyther for church or commonwealth. If the people be governors, who shall be governed? As for monarchy, and aristocracy, they are both of them clearly approoved, and directed in scripture, yet so as referreth the soveraigntie to himselfe, and setteth up Theocracy in both, as the best forme of government in the commonwealth, as well as in the church.*

Being criticized for the intolerance and departing

from the spirit of Puritan Fathers who fled persecution in England, Samuel Willard, pastor of Old South Church in Boston, wrote:

> *I perceive that they are mistaken in the design of our first Planters, whose business was not Toleration; but were professed Enemies of it.*

Jonathan Winthrop, one of the founders of the Puritan Massachusetts Bay Colony, criticized Nathaniel Ward, a fellow clergyman and author of the first constitution in North America, The Massachusetts Body of Liberties, for his admiration of the Classical legacy, rightfully seeing this as a contradiction to the Biblical account:

> *In his sermon he delivered many useful things, but in a moral and political discourse, grounding his propositions much upon the old Roman and Grecian governments, which sure is an error... Among other things, he advised the people to keep all their magistrates in an equal rank, and not give more honor or power to one than another, which is easier to advise than to prove, seeing it is against the practice of Israel.*

This is a pretty soft statement, considering that the Puritan writer, John Milton, in his *Paradise Lost*, made the fallen angels the adepts of classical and philosophical virtues, and that it is Satan who delivers the speech about equality and liberty, while angels Raphael and Abdiel preach obedience.

In contrast to the popular belief in the prominent role of Puritans in the Founding, two thirds of the Constitution Convention delegates belonged to a more tolerant Church of England (Pangle & Pangle 1993, 21, 23–25, 27).

Being understandably shy of their name during and after the Revolutionary War, Anglicans renamed themselves as Episcopalians. Moderation of the Church of England, or Episcopal Church, balanced by the reasonable inhibition of the activity of the radical, fundamentalist Catholics and Calvinist sects, was praised by many Enlightenment thinkers, such as Montesquieu, David Hume and Adam Smith (Pangle & Pangle 1993, 20). The tolerance of the Episcopal Church can be seen up to the present day—with women and openly gay bishops among its clergy.

Many Framers are even hard to call Christians in the full sense of the word, because they were greatly affected by Deist philosophy and Free Masonic ideas. Former Anglicans Washington, Jefferson, Madison, Monroe, and former Puritans, John Adams and Franklin changed from the religious views of their childhood and youth and embraced Deism. Thomas Paine, who represented a radical wing of the Deist movement, which viewed Christianity as a barrier to moral improvement, befriended Franklin, Jefferson, Adams and Washington, and was a close friend of James Monroe. He lived in Monroe's house during the 1790s, when he moved to France to assist the French Revolution (Monroe was serving as a minister in Paris at the time). When Paine was arrested during the French Reign of Terror, Monroe applied all his influence to free him from prison. Long months there took a heavy toll on Paine's health, and he spent two years recuperating at Monroe's home.

Deists differed from the traditional Judeo-Christian concept of God. Instead of a Hebrew God named YHWH, who had revealed himself to Moses on Mount Sinai, the God of Abraham, Isaac, Jacob, Joseph, David, Solomon, the Prophets, and Jesus of Nazareth, they postulated a distant deity, which they named by terms we may find in the Declaration of Independence: "Nature's God", "Creator", "Supreme Judge", and "Divine Providence". (Holmes 2006, 36, 41, 47)

THE COLLAPSE OF THE ARISTOCRATIC CONSTITUTION

However, as time passes, elites are changing. Today's elites of "the rich and the well-born", who guide the "mass of turbulent and changing people", hold ideals far detached from the ones of the Founding Fathers. The best manifestation of this change is the recent "reaffirmation" of the national motto "In God We Trust" by Congress by a stunningly alarming vote of 396 to 9. In reality, this move has not only reaffirmed the disrespect for the ideals of the Founding Fathers, who, in 1782, came up with the completely different motto, "E Pluribus Unum", which lasted until the "Red Scare" campaign of 1956, but also violated the Constitution itself, establishing primacy of a religion, and the particular one, in government affairs.

The new elites represent that which the Founding Fathers wished to guard our Republic against, with their "Aristocratic Constitution"—the moral heirs of uneducated and unenlightened forces which convicted and sentenced Socrates to death almost two and a half millennia ago, or founded and shaped the religiously totalitarian Massachusetts Colony, with its practices of literal and hyperbolic Witch Hunts.

Thomas E. Patterson, professor of Government and Press at Harvard University, in his essay, "The Vanishing Voter", points out that the Civil War was effectively a *coup d'état*, when the big financial and business elites had dismantled the Jeffersonian and Hamiltonian governing system, where the state was protecting the interests of the weak and less fortunate, and established a system where profit was put above all other interests. The Calvinist sects were valuable allies in this revolt:

> *The idea of a free market seemed vaguely like the principle of self-reliance, which enabled small-town businessmen and Protestant churchgoers to embrace the Republican philosophy nearly as whole.*
>
> (Patterson 2003, 28)

This ideological union was able to refute the attacks of the Progressivists at the end of the nineteenth century and beginning of the twentieth. Only the Great Depression and World War II made possible a brief return of the Progressivists' ideas in the form of the New Deal, until they were overtaken once again by the "Reagan Revolution". (Patterson 2003, 30–35)

There should be no doubts that the use (or rather misuse) of the taming and guiding "back door" mechanisms of the Constitution by the new elites will be, at the very least, unhelpful for preserving Liberty and Justice.

A handful of Supreme Court rulings over the last few years show how: the Citizens United case gave corporations a "personhood" and protection of the Bill of Rights; the Westboro Baptist Church case reaffirmed the "right" of religious hate speech; the Lavoni T. Kid case confirmed the unaccountability of officials for their unlawful actions; and Justice Scalia commented during the Troy Davis case to the effect that the execution of the innocent is not unconstitutional.

The new elites no longer carry a Republican Spirit, not even the Aristocratic Republican one of the Founders. Today's elites, akin to their Puritan predecessors at the time of Founding, are preoccupied with ideas of Middle Eastern origin regarding the herding of "sheeple". Montesquieu noted that this Spirit is capable of producing only Despotism (Pangle 2010, 38–50).

There is no need for a sudden, precipitous political change. Using the exploits of the Founders' "Aristocratic Constitution", without their Enlightened Spirit, it is just a matter of political skill to migrate to what a French thinker Alexis de Tocqueville, who visited and praised the US at the beginning of the nineteenth century, called "Soft Despotism":

I see an innumerable multitude of men, alike and equal, who turn about without repose in order to procure for themselves petty and vulgar pleasures with which they fill their souls. Each of them, withdrawn apart, is a virtual stranger, unaware of the fate of the others: his children and his particular friends form for him the entirety of the human race; as for his fellow citizens, he is beside them but he sees them not;

he touches them and senses them not; he exists only in himself and for himself alone, and, if he still has a family, one could say at least that he no longer has a fatherland.

Over these is elevated an immense, tutelary power, which takes sole charge assuring their enjoyment and watching over their fate... the sovereign extends its arms about the society as a whole; it covers its surface with a network of petty regulations—complicated, minute, and uniform—through which even the most original minds and the most vigorous souls know not how to make their way past the crowd and emerge into the light of day. It does not break wills; it softens them, bends them, and directs them; rarely does it force one to act, but it constantly opposes itself to one's acting on one's own; it does not destroy, it prevents things from being born; it does not tyrannize, it gets in the way: it curtails, it enervates, it extinguishes, it stupefies, and finally it reduces each nation to nothing more than a herd of timid and industrious animals, of which the government is the shepherd.

(Tocqueville 2011, 244)

People cease to be citizens involved in a continuous civic discourse, exchange and testing of ideas. They become cautious, and scared of voicing their thoughts through fear of persecution, because of the constantly popping up of new taboos (take a recent "soft persecution" of the veteran journalist Helen Thomas). People become isolated and start to think they are the only bad sheep in the herd, and, feeling lonely and hopeless, let the new elites do what they please.

In the end, paradoxically, despite the unruly, wild, and sometimes dark nature of the unabridged freedom of speech and the press, it is the only hope and guard left against our nation sliding into Tocqueville's "Soft Despotism".

BIBLIOGRAPHY

Hamilton, Alexander, John Jay, and James Madison, *The Essential Federalist and Anti-Federalist Papers*. New York: Classic Books America, 2009

Hamilton, Alexander, "Speech on the Constitutional Convention on a Plan of Government." In *Selected Writings and Speeches of Alexander Hamilton*, edited by Morton J. Frisch. Washington, D.C.: American Enterprise Institute, 1985

Holmes, David, *The Faith of the Founding Fathers*. New York: Oxford University Press, 2006

Montesquieu, Baron de (Charles de Secondat), *Considerations on the Causes of the Greatness of the Romans and Their Decline*. Indianapolis: Hackett Publishing Company, 1999

Pangle, Lorraine S., and Thomas Pangle, *The Learning of Liberty: The Educational Ideas of the American Founders*. Lawrence: University Press of Kansas, 1993

Pangle, Thomas, *The Theological Basis of Liberal Modernity in Montesquieu's "Spirit of the laws"*. Chicago: University of Chicago Press, 2010

Patterson, Thomas E., *The Vanishing Voter: Public Involvement in an Age of Uncertainty*. New York: Vintage Books, 2003

Plato, "Republic." In *The Republic of Plato: Translated, with Notes and an Interpretive Essay*. Translated by Allan Bloom. New York: Basic Books, 1991

Rush, Benjamin, "A Plan for the Establishment of Public Schools." In *American Political Writing during the Founding Era 1760-1805,*Vol. 1 by Charles S. Hyneman and Donald S. Lutz. Indianapolis: Liberty Fund, 1983

Tocqueville, Alexis de, *Democracy in America: Volume 2*. New York: Quill Pen Classics, 2008

Welter, Rush, *Popular Education and Democratic Thought in America*. New York: Columbia University Press, 1962

ABOUT THE AUTHOR

Stanislaw Sielicki is a history, political philosophy and comparative mythology enthusiast. He was writing short forms on the Internet before the terms "blogger", "social networking" and "Web forums" were invented. If you are familiar with such names and abbreviations as Usenet, Fido or BBS, you have got the idea.

His motto is "If you are 100 percent, positively sure that a particular historical event developed in a certain way, it is the time to carefully and rigorously check your sources!"

EDITORIAL REVIEW

What were the Classical Philosophers and Thinkers of the Age of Enlightenment saying about the Censorship and Freedom of Speech? What did the Founding Fathers learn from their Great Predecessors?

Were the Framers of the Constitution the real Champions of Freedom? Of whom were the Founders afraid when they planted back-doors and exploits in their Constitution? What has changed since the times of the Founding?

This short essay may help you find answers to the questions mentioned above.

FRONT COVER

Witches Of Salem: Trial of Giles Corey. Artist: C. S. Reinhardt.

www.ingramcontent.com/pod-product-compliance
Lightning Source LLC
Chambersburg PA
CBHW061233280526
45784CB00006B/2748